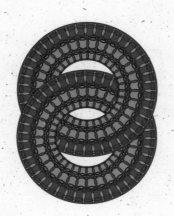

RATTLE

POEMS ELOISE BRUCE

RATTLE

POEMS ELOISE BRUCE

CavanKerry ◊ Press LTD.

Library of Congress Cataloging-in-Publication Data

Bruce, Eloise.
   Rattle : poems / by Eloise Bruce.
      p. cm.
   ISBN 0-9707186-8-3
      I. Title.
 PS3602.R83R38 2004
 811'.54—dc21

                                        2003042888

Cover Illustration: "Untitled" © 1999 Sam Goodsell
Author Photograph by Angela Lloyd
Cover and Book Design by Peter Cusack

First Edition

Printed in the United States of America

CavanKerry Press Ltd.
Fort Lee, New Jersey
www.cavankerrypress.org

ACKNOWLEDGMENTS

Acknowledgment is gratefully made to the editors of the following publications where these poems first appeared: *American Letters and Commentary*, "They Have No More for the Land"; *Blue Moon Review*, "Out of the Same Salty Sea, To Michael"; *The Paterson Literary Review*, "What Happened to the Foot-Washing Baptist"; *GSL* (Northern Ireland), "The Wreck"; *The Journal of New Jersey Poets*, "The Day We Said So"; *Stet* (Ireland) "Queen Maeve" (as "Under the Influence of Colored Objects"); *US1 Worksheets*, "Our Jazz," "The Warbler's Song," "Dear M," "Cat Fishing," "Latitudinal"; *US1: The Newspaper*, "Community Garden, Lawrenceville, New Jersey."

I am grateful to The Frost Place, to Landmark Education, and to the New Jersey State Council on the Arts for their support, which enabled me to write this book, and to all of my friends and family for their encouragement. I especially would like to acknowledge Carol Sheehan, David Keller, and each of the Cool Women, who have been careful readers of these poems, and Jean Valentine, my extraordinary teacher. I also wish to thank Baron Wormser for his editorial assistance and Joan Handler for her belief in, and enthusiasm for, this book.

**NATIONAL
ENDOWMENT
FOR THE ARTS**

CavanKerry Press is grateful to the the National Endowment for the Arts for its support of this book.

For David Keller

*Come from the four winds, O breath,
and breathe upon these slain, that
they may live.*

Ezekiel 37:9

CONTENTS

III. THEY CARRY THE STORIES

Foreword

My friend Eloise Bruce's *Rattle* is a book of poems charged equally by the spirits of pleasure and pain; of "stories beyond number" from a Southern childhood in the American past recalled and improvised and conjured by a poet in love with the world's sounds, "the emphatic hurry, hurry, hurry" of the warbler, and of the rattle.

It is true the rattle is Death's—the snake in the garden, the recurrent nightmare, the body fighting for breath—theatrical and absolute. But it is also the instrument made by this poet from a living gourd in her real garden. Its sound is of longing and dread both realized in the astonishment of love.

Bruce begins by blending creation tale with Genesis, positing her story as a traditional one of origin and exile. Here, she'll sing in the face of darkness. Her poems will proliferate in a domestic daydream, just before dawn, where "words wait" and feeling sharpens, where memory awakens and poems repopulate the landscape, create a genealogy. Then the world is as it was and is: Segregation, divorce, accident, abortion, corrupt authority, false religion, the unending never and always of father and mother, love not lived; the deaths of everyone. Yet, Bruce rejects traditional elegy, the catharsis of confession. Her poems link writing instead to an originating act, shedding new light on the water, breathing new life into the familial house, where the abandonments of childhood become the amazements of marriage; fear of death becomes knowledge of self.

She will say what happens, but according to her music, "this hum, tongue, ruffle, fortissimo is / (that keeps) the air in and around us jumping," is part Southern blarney, part Northern jazz. Just as she'll "place" her husband "at the heart of her people," evoking the connection between burial and birth, Bruce joins oral traditions to literary ones—sestina to the blues,

Baptist hymn to wandering monologue. Her ear is for this minute, for the body, for your voice and mine; for the absent, the beloved, the hilarious, the perverse. Even her dog's essential murderousness is sung, because it is Being. For her, not the elegist's art of memory and consolation, but the storyteller's art of engendering.

"If we had a keen vision and feeling of all ordinary human life," George Eliot wrote in *Middlemarch*, "it would be like hearing the grass grow and the squirrel's heartbeat, and we should die of that roar which lies on the other side of silence." Anyone who has felt unendurable grief, or the beauty of creation, knows something of this dying. The poems of *Rattle* know we would live, too, listening and telling.

Julie Agoos

QUEEN MAEVE

Dreaming within these walls all night,
we woke with both eyes open,
barely winking at the morning light.

We shower and sing with the long-legged fly.
Queen Maeve keeps time in the attic,
and the pig-keepers roar in the toy box below stairs.

Turn out the lamp whose fringe rhymes with *orange*.
Our words wait in sun-melted butter.
We'll eat our troubles with bubbling metaphor,
punctuate the teapot with boiling time,
hang the wash out on the line.

Today, we'll scrub and paint the walls
using colors we don't yet recognize.
The key in the door shines.
Come in. The poem is just here. Come inside.

I
MY PEOPLE

WIFE AND HUSBAND

At first, darkness, except for the stars
until the heavens invented the sea,
until the stars discovered the blue of sky.

The sea was the blue of sea, the land sat at its side,
and once imagined, she and he lived at the water's edge
where the sun spread endlessly, end over endless summer.

The wind hissed in the grass and she
thought of the serpent, Adam's face in a cloud,
and hers a small shadow in his image on the land.

When the stars fell that night, she flung them back,
recognized the heavens and knew they had made her.
She carved what she knew into a stone.

He helped her drag it to the headland
where they raised it to catch the moon's face.
There were other stones and the birth of children,

then came the lunatic winds that drove the trees mad,
dancing some from the ground, then
the icy aloneness and our stories beyond number.

DAVID

Just there between Bynie and Doc,
my father and his father,
I watched the leaves fall off a catalpa
all at once because that's the way it happens,
no stranger than orgasm, birth, kisses,
hunger, rage, a name, or a death.

My people are Tyla, Jasper, Willie, Margaret,
and Louella who fed and cared for us all.
My people are quick to judge and mostly generous,
like Great-Aunt Maude and my married cousins.
They love their past best, my Lily, Nina,
Aileen, Norma Jean, Byron, Althea, and the many Homers.
I place you here, David, at the heart of my people,
for I know our love story but not theirs.

You are one of life's sweetest discoveries,
as astonishing as my first hearing the beat of a heart.
I slept on my great-grandmother Eloise's breast.
Her heart pounded in my sleep so loudly
I opened my eyes, we sat up and were startled.

Visiting your people, I found you one Christmas Eve
waiting at the door in your Tom Mix hat.
It was you, a white snake in black felt,
it was you-we holding the gift
of *will be*, on a cold rainy night in Summertown.

DARK WHITE BLUES

Moonless at midnight Daddy out on the lake
with his gig and Rayovac flashlight. I hum
like yesterday's fried chicken, no ear
for music. I am tone deaf as the frogs
we will kill and eat for tomorrow's supper.
Mother sleeps in the rock house dreaming of beagles.

She cried with Daddy's nasty passel of beagles
all this afternoon, while we floated on the lake,
the crickets and cicadas relentlessly humming,
mosquitoes buzzing the same note in our ears
as the croaking of the splashing bullfrogs
who search with bulging eyes for their supper.

Momma lost the baby last night after supper
and screamed in tune with the howls of Daddy's beagles.
This place is poison, the water moccasins and this lake,
she finally spoke, flat as you please, no hum,
no melody, little breath left, no ears,
no eyes, a kind of death with frogs.

In Sunday school they told me about the locusts and the frogs,
and I'm looking at their legs and thinking of plagues for supper.
The teacher didn't say anything about a plague of beagles,
I muse, as we carry our frogleg and green tomato picnic down
            to the lake.
Dusk again and as we eat, the insects begin to hum
the blues of our lives into our waiting ears.

Momma spoke to Daddy, *For Christ sake, open your ears.*
We let them fill up with the lamentation of the frogs.
Like Lady Day wailing hungry for love and they for supper.
Like the Blind Boys of Alabama, Daddy's beagles
hit a sweet harmony. Even the lake
offers a soft base, more than humming.

Our stomachs no longer rumble, growl, or hum,
but our hearts are as empty as our ears
are full. You know how the sound suddenly stops? A frog
belts a lonely lyric, hungry for the dead and her supper,
the backup and the slow chorus from Momma and the beagles.
Tomorrow she will load us in the car and leave Daddy and the lake.

MAMA TAUGHT ME

Tennessee Williams got it wrong;
Grits and grillades are good.

Mama always looks her best
wrapped in a mess of words
sitting on a veranda.

Never marry a pig farmer.
Live next to an ocean.

She prefers a background of slaves
and live oak, hung with Spanish moss,
just like Vivien Leigh as Scarlett.

If a lie makes a good story, it becomes truth.
A fool's money can be yours.

But exactly like Blanche Dubois,
the story always ends with what we had then
that we don't have now.

Margaret Mitchell got it right.
Blood binds; the dead stick around.

Lately, the thin line between her
and our dead ancestors has grown mighty hazy.
I am careful to be somewhere in the future.

Southern women have eyelashes, tongues,
and claws made of the softest stuff.

Childless, just out of reach, I put Mama
into poems with lines like *Loving Mama is kin
to waiting in a cloud of mosquitoes.*

Drink makes life bearable.
Live facing the past.

Mama never had a pot to piss in.
She misses money as if it were a dead relation.
Mama is my kith. Poor Mama, giving birth to a poet
who knows a lime tree is the truth.

Children cause unbearable pain.
A lime tree is a treasure.

RELATIONS

Twenty-five years ago my great-uncle and aunt
lived on this lake with cows and blackberry bushes,
all gone to scruffy woods now, ablaze this fall
as John Michael and Patsy spread Daddy's ashes
off the dam. We all feast on turnip greens, catfish
and hush puppies in the home place turned

restaurant, sipping ice tea, the fried food turns
my husband's Yankee stomach. My aunt
Marjorie sits opposite, delicate with her filet of fish,
my father's steely hair on her head and bushy
eyebrows above her dark eyes, and Granny's ashen
circles beneath. I am the sin-eater and we are fallen.

I am surprised they have chosen me to take the fall;
the bad first child of the first wife took her turn
to read T. S. Eliot and not the Bible. *Ashes to ashes*
recites the able second wife's child, Suzy. My aunt
has stopped directly addressing me. Perky and bushy-
tailed Suzy charms, and I am a flapping fish

out of water. She, abundant as Jesus' loaves and fishes
and actually speaking in parables. My face fallen,
I could flop into the cool under a nearby bush,
lie in the dirt and think of the *turn, turn, turn*
of this and all seasons in the verse my aunt
reads, then rise restored from the dark and ashes

like Cinderella or a phoenix out of my own ashes.
Jesus said to the apostles, *I will make you fishers
of men.* I am drowning in my own blood, the aunt
and the cousins. They might, any minute, fall
to their knees and pray, all heads upward, turned
to heaven and me still looking for a burning bush

to guide me out of the wilderness of this ambush.
I push through the undergrowth, to find the ashes
of my father floating in the lake. Grief will turn
to winter, spring, summer, and another fall.
We all become dust one day, food for the fishes
or the worms, some sooner than others. My aunt

will return to God to join my father who loved to fish.
He caught bushels before his gray bone and ash
scattered this fall, untouched by our last blood aunt.

OUT OF THE
SAME SALTY SEA:
TO MICHAEL

There is the cooler you stole from Inga,
the pup tent you took from our brother's garage,
and your little boat baked to dry rot.

If you find enough sand dollars each day,
you will be able to buy the cold beer
to keep yourself from cooking through.

Out of the salty sea, alive
you bring those dollars, green, furry, and soft-shelled,
staining your fingers with iodine, salt's age-old friend.

We all live under the same heavens;
in your part of the world everything bakes—
the seaweed, your back, the sea foam and palmettos.

If your boat springs a leak, you are sunk
in the sea, whose bay holds the tiny island
where you live, the tide, your clock, rising twice a day.

Twice a day the squall line passes through.
You piss in the sea. In season hurricanes come.
You keep yourself drunk with no steady companion.

The water is warm as a bath.
It has sharks in its shallows and sand dollars
just under the salty sand. The air will cook you.

Your island is often covered at high tide,
you mutter to the wind, the sun and the moon and water.
They naturally conspire to kill you.

Be vigilant or your sand dollars will be stolen.
Mind the ancient water and her minions,
more flow than ebb. She is drawn to you.

THE WITCH UNDER MY BED

The autopsy discovered residue,
a glistening ocean in her lungs;
no spider webs or shadows,
her stomach full of tiny patches of moonlight
and the remains of the light in my eyes.

In her skull, the glint
of a dark-drunken memory,
      faint voices illusive, foxfire
      and brief glimpses of the flesh
      of my mother and her lovers,
      and the flicker of candlelight.

I was amazed at the finding
of glowworms and fireflies
still alive in her womb.

When the night was pulled
from her mouth, her last words,
I am afraid of the light,
flew like sparks in the face.

Recorded: her only distinguishing mark,
my name tattooed inside a blazing sun
next to the dark heart in her chest.

If I had known her demons,
I would have been brave,
grabbing my own uncovered foot
with my own someday-to-be-withered hand,
and climbed under the bed with her,
chanting and cooing.

THE SOLID BODY

June spreads like butter.
I am a white smudge in its heat.
I know this melody and the crickets' music,
their back legs moving so fast.
I sometimes fall or fly
or am transported by tornados in my dreams.

I am ten, I am chubby, and I am running.
My feet and his pound over the hard red clay.
I jump the sty, into the blackberries,
in three long leaps. The briars and his belt lash me.
He is slower because of the drink.
He carries me through the long rows of pecan trees.
I lie so still after doing the daddy dance.

THE KIDNAPPING

I recollect people from my childhood
as smudges with a hint of features
like the sketches of jurors in some murder trial

I recall the acne-scarred cheek
or the mole on the chin   nothing more
the same with places
I've shunned the past   until lately

It might be the smell of beer and bacon
or the way my daddy's smile translates
onto my brother's face and I am
mounting those familiar porch steps
only to find shadow where a front room used to be

On that dim yesterday
                  my father
a young man sits smiling on an erasure
of a chair I once knew   Outside on a street
his car vague except for its fins   waits

In the days that followed
                  my brother
Ron and I stand at a murky location
There is that old dread like a wound that is to come
The car rushes toward us   Behind the windshield
it is filled with eyes   They are on us
Suddenly my father's smile and hands engulf Ron
snatching only him into the car
Maxie and her children Twig and Patsy
inside crystal clear   The car is full
The engine revs   chrome
blurring to gray   I am alone
in a spill of lies   a smear
a murmur   I'm an abbreviation

WHAT HAPPENED TO
THE FOOT-WASHING BAPTIST

The bad boy poured a handful of soot
into the toes of his daddy's Sunday shoes,
and though it has been on my mind for days
I can't recall many more details
—the church floor's color or my granny's face—
but can recall tiny things: her clip-ons,
the little pencils, the tithing envelopes,
my granddaddy's gray-striped seersucker suit
with a drop of scrambled eggs on the lapel,
the preacher's fists raised to a ceiling
as high as heaven, and I know
angels might have lived in that church
if the wrath of God hadn't gotten there first.
No sane angel would risk the threat of brimstone
which could erupt at any second.
Praying for their own salvation,
the choir sang to be washed in the blood of the lamb.
The preacher said to rise up or be smote.
I didn't like the sound of either much. I sat tight,
breathing the cool air and nothing happened,
no blood or fire. Just that preacher hollering,
about to reveal his dirty feet,
and me hoping for just one angel.

THE PUNCH LINE

And the preacher said, *Shut your damn mouth, Woman!*
That's fish you see. At a Saturday night supper
somewhere in my childhood I heard my first joke.

Daddy, I haven't seen you in twenty-five years,
imagine my surprise at receiving your letter:

> *Eloise, have you accepted Jesus as your savior?*
> *Remember, sins don't send you to Hell;*
> *NOT believing does.*

First Man and First Woman left the underworld.
They came to the earth through a hollow reed.
They found a girl child.
She gave them the land between four mountains
and four rivers. The people rose from her skin.
When she rubbed her right armpit,
the Bitterwater Clan was born.

The joke goes like this:
A woman is being baptized in a lake.
After the first dunk, she cries out,
Jesus! I see Jesus.
Then the preacher says the part about the fish.

He wrote,
> *Hell is full of good people.*
> *But if you believe that Jesus died on the Cross*
> *for you and me and he will come again*
> *to take us to Heaven, you are saved.*

Please favor me with a reply.
How can the punch line be *Shut your damn mouth, Woman*?

From Angel Peak, the girl child watches the Glittering World,
Monster Slayer, Child Born of Water, and Beauty
in the House of Dawn.

SCRAPBOOK 1973

1.

Henry is long in every way—
tooth, his hair, penis, and silences.
He is eating buttermilk and cornbread
or oyster stew. He wants a divorce.

I wanted to have sex, make a baby,
be married my whole life.
He thinks I am crazy, dangerous,
unfit to raise his child.

2.

The principal's paddle cracks
on the buttocks of my homeroom student.
The boy is white, the man is black,
I am gray and small in my skin,
hungover with a mouth full of bile.

3.

The preacher plugs my nose with his thumb
and forefinger, pushing me backward
into the baptismal. I still feel desperate
and cannot find God. I am cold.

4.

The bitch's uterus has come out with the pups.
My father-in-law will let her die. No hope,
Henry shoots her with his rifle. His mother
and sister dig the hole before supper.

1959, AND ALL
THEY HAD DONE FOR US

A friend of mine snarled at me,
But we all loved our mammies.
I wanted to growl, *But did they love us?*

If she and all the others loved them so,
where were the odes, leather-bound volumes
in sets as large as encyclopedias?

If we simply loved them, clung to them
as all young cling to their mothers,
then why should I be the one to range around,
sniffing at something long buried?

Perhaps it is because of the nature of love,
how it will survive in the heart for as long as it can.
Sometimes it lives as long as the body.

In the way seasons turn, with the certain deaths
and the birth of babies and tender sprouts,
Selma was far down the road
and it was further still to Birmingham.
I, just a little girl, spent my days
floating pale as a magnolia blossom
in a crystal bowl of water, oblivious
as if I lived on the buffet with the silver.

Margaret kept me fed and watered.
Luella polished the silver.
Jasper cut the grass, and
when they were good, my mama
would say *I love them like family.*
But I really did, blindly and fully;
I loved Margaret and I ache for her still
as Persephone longs for Demeter.

I longed to be Margaret's nut-brown child
resting my cheek on her thigh
while she plaited my hair in long rows.
I still long for her.
I'd like for her to dwell on me, too,
as the light returns, while she rests on her porch
sipping a long tall glass of buttermilk and honey.

But remembering is its own kind of bondage
that I couldn't wish for her.
We have feasted on the pomegranate,
sucking the sweet flesh from the seeds
and swallowing them so they rest in our bellies even now.
Our world is still draped in bougainvillea to hide our stench.

In the half-light of memory I walk
through the rooms and down the dirt street,
to the place where my momma scolds,
And after all we've done for you.
Margaret must have done something bad,

eyes on her feet, quiet.
Who was that dusty child
dressed in hand-me-down clothes?

It baffled me to think of her with a life
outside of us. Where there was real jazz
and juba and other children to love.

Margaret married a man named Ham.
They had a dozen children,
and when I take warm cornbread
from the oven and eat it with lots of butter,
I take them into myself deeply:

digesting the sorrows, the songs, the horrors
and the hallelujahs. I walk until my feet ache

with plenty; and then dance to a frenzy,
jostling the seeds that shake and rattle inside my body,

finally to lay my head down
on the earth's great brown and dimpled thigh.
I sink in like roots, like spring rain, a celebrant again.

THE WRECK

To themselves they are the big brothers.
Their shamans are called momma.
Selected by divination at birth,
spending their childhoods cloistered
in caves, they envision
the world into which they emerge at age nine.
The entries of their ancient, uninhabited cities
are marked by maps
of their own spiritual geography.

So I have carved my own landscape?
A graceful line to age eight,
followed by a deep gorge,
punctuation and reminder of
December 26, 1957,
Bing Crosby on the radio,
Daddy singing along.
We drank 7-Ups with
Planter's peanuts dropped down the spout,
my little brother wetting
Woody Woodpecker tattoos
from the bottle's condensation
and applying them to our arms.
The rain was coming down in Phoenix City.
We were just passing the Bamboo Motel
when it all happened in slow motion:
the car,
the eyes
behind
the wipers,
straight at us.
The roar and
glass,
in slivers,
piercing

my skin.
I screamed until . . .
a new line radiated from the center wound,
after a break. The new line became a rough fracture
in which my little brother grew to be a cocaine dealer.
In the side's hairline fractures, I grew my fat armor,
and daddy became unrecognizable in his desperation.
All our tears were blood when he pulled his boy
from the floorboards of the car,
hemorrhaging from mouth, nose, ears, and eyes.

II
HUM, TONGUE, RUFFLE

SEASCAPE

My hand, the shell of a ghost-crab,
cracked open when I slapped my father's face.
I mistook my hand for a bird, a sandpiper.
That I struck my father is not as important
as it is for us to keep our eyes on our hands.

I glove mine in desire
to write, take pleasure, maim, or bestow.
In the language of desire, my own hand
can command the fingers of my left
to scurry into the sea while the remaining ones
fly up at sunset. This is not a fiction;
the bones of our hands remember
forbidden fruit and the discovery of fire.

In February on the beach of my virginity,
I warm my hands over burning driftwood.
My middle-aged self has been writing of our hands,
how her fingers moved, soft as feathers
over her lover's skin. Our hands will be warm.

The weather is wild. The wind whips my hair.
Sparks rise in bursts toward heaven.
I am yesterday, perfectly longing for tomorrow.

BAPTIZED

(for Doc Long)

It's hot today, so hot
even the devil's thinking of getting dunked.
God winks, Satan
sets angels in flight
and lays his crazy collection of wings
out on the sidewalk for all to see.
You're chillin, all put together
like cream and sugar in a cup of black coffee,
and thinking it's possible to steal from him.

Whiff of collards and fried chicken,
we've been down by Speckle Red's
all day looking for those angels, and I been standing round
all pink and pale and now I know
the color of the devil's skin. Satan might look just like
my aunt Maude or my daddy's buddy Otis.

Our poems are the space between us and God.
In your dream a woman jumped down the devil's throat.
You've been teaching me how to laugh at the devil.

I've been traveling down
a big wide boulevard too long
and just so I don't have to go down
to that dusty crossroad
where the blues wail,
where the devil's dealing,
and I'll have to meet my flesh face-to-face.

You are all cool, it's so hot, you're gonna
divert the devil's attention,
steal us those wings, we are gonna fly.

THE VIEW FROM MERRILL LYNCH

The occasional feather parachutes,
while I recollect from thirty-nine floors up
that madness runs in my family
and I am a Southerner, no excuse to explain away
my grandfather watering banana plants in his boxer shorts.

On the ride up with my Yankee mother-in-law,
I am thinking how most of my relations
wouldn't have been allowed on the elevator.
Like my little brother, the Sand Dollar Sea Captain,
who has eaten too many mushrooms
and claims all of the sand dollars
around Anna Maria Island as his own.

When we finally descend to the street,
we watch a child holding his mother's hand.
She could be wishing for her sweet boy
the life my husband's mother desired
for him, to revere her from left of center,
while having a magnificent job
that will change the world,
while he avoids ever being arrested.
I didn't have children,
fearing my own bad chemistry.

My own mother has often said to us, *Never
have children; they will break your heart.*
When the moon is full,
she takes her broken heart out on the porch,
opens her purse and yells at the moon.
For money-luck, she always told us children.
Maybe her problem is one of geography;
the moon is just too far away.

THE DAY WE SAID SO
(for David)

They lived there when their son killed himself;
a lot was wrong before, but got much worse.
She was unhappy with her husband,
so much so, that even after fifty years
her sadness is still tangible in the old place.
The house, somehow unworthy of care,
has lost any bright hue; the windows have gone grey.
I won't marry in this pale house,
though the view would make our wedding album.

Her husband hardly worked this land at all,
only occasionally going to the barn for a tool.
He bought the place for the view of the notch in the mountains.
That was many years ago now, long enough to be history.
Her husband was a poet, so he did work the land after all,
with words like *woods, farmhouse near,*
bitter bark, good fences, touch, and *hand.*

I will marry you in his barn with the doors of the house closed,
the curtains drawn over the colorless windows.
Before, you will chain-smoke outside the open barn doors,
peering in at our bright decorations. So handsome
in your panama suit, white bucks, and sweet pink face,
you will join me in the barn and we will marry,
our eyes fixed on the clear blue sky and the notch,
rising over the house and the woods, and our hands touching.

OUR JAZZ

This morning after you spoke a word,
I took the "o" out and rubbed its lotion
on my body. I carefully stored the consonants;
exact meaning could be important someday.

When you are angry and closemouthed,
I have no breath. I have no tonic to fill me.
Fear furnished the silent rooms of my youth
where my parents quietly hated each other.
No sound throbbed between them.
My prince would arrive with some noise and jingle.

From the very start, I collected vowel sounds.
I garnished our meals with them.
There were so many, I began adorning our clothes.
Your chat and skin kept my ears ringing.

I spread diphthongs on the bed after we married
and painted long vowels onto the walls.
Now, we take showers in the "ah's" and sow the "ee's"
in our garden. When we have an abundance,
we make gifts for friends, thick scarves knitted
with bits of complaints and arguments
and the sighs of Saturday morning lovemaking.

Sometimes it is hard for me to keep my bearings.
I fold punctuation into the pages of reference books.
I want to know where the end-stops are.
I know one is certain to be at the end of us;
until then, there is this resonance in our bones.
This hum, tongue, ruffle, fortissimo
keeps the air in and around us jumping.

MYSTERY IN THE FLORIDA ROOM

How would we look to Nancy Drew
through our jalousies, like slides
smeared with some ooze for magnification?

Mother in her housedress mostly,
us slapping each other mostly,
while the Mickey Mouse Club droned.

What would she make of us and the roaches,
the Seagrams 7, progressive jazz?
In chapter Thirteen, Nancy might explain

my mother setting her mattress on fire,
the drapes going up and shining in the glass,
the coral snakes, my mother's absent lover,
and, close to the end of the book, the part
where mother goes to that butcher in Miami.

My mother taught Nancy Drew to avoid
the nasty. Nancy is made of words,
I of flesh. I write *flame and blood.*

My mother left the girl-fetus in Little Havana
and forgot her, but she still comes
to me in dreams, sometimes as Nancy, sometimes as a
        reflection.

The language of her may be fiction, but I
am her mother now. I pen our existence,
hanging the words from my hair: *sutra, stele, vervain.*

I loop them around the soft skin of my toes: *rune,
lotus, cairn.* I swallow and inhale them,
pollen, salt, and *sister.*

GOBLETS

My neighbor Helen arrives aflutter.
Had I whispered to her last evening
out in the yard? No, I had not.

Shall I tell her someone breathed my name
in the twilight and I thought of fairies?
I look into her great-grandmother eyes.

All day I have been seeking sparkles
at the edge of my vision, shadows of wings,
with my ear cocked for buzzing and whispers.

Could they lighten the burden of her junkie son?
Would they take away my long grief?
Her eyes are filled with dread.

The folk have thrown fairy dust in them,
and she has forgotten all but a canny echo.
So, she is spared the fright of a changeling child.

I saw one years ago in Odessa, otherworldly,
his features and limbs pointed and too thin.
The folk, as much, a kind of insect,

are easy to see with a child's eye.
I sigh with loneliness and recall
the opalescence of tiny eyes.

We are two working-class women in New Jersey
with fairies in the back of our gardens.
Helen can't remember, and I can't forget.

Long ago, when I lay under the porch steps,
goblets and goblets of rain poured,
while a sylph covered my cheeks with dewy kisses.

WAITING FOR YOU
(for David)

A man dances by with a birdcage on his foot. Two women,
one with such long happy legs, pass by the glass. I wait
for you at the Gamut, just off Park Avenue.

A woman carrying tears goes past too slowly,
a man in a mask of worry and another whose feet
whisper and mostly do not touch the sidewalk at all.

I sit facing the Victorian sofa, just like my Granny's, heart-
shaped, but dressed in blue not red. On it, a couple, my age,
neck, two women. A boy stands outside the window
staring in. He has candy to sell. I am waiting for you

late and in winter. You will come soon, fast,
face-first, like a bud ready to unfold. There you are,
approaching with a whole new season in your pockets,

and when the waitress thinks you are merely paying
for your coffee, spring flows from her hand onto the floor
and toward the feet near and far.
I am humming love songs, all of them at once.

A CHINESE LANTERN

One afternoon in what the Buddha
calls my future, I sat on a bench,
gazing at a painting of a gray line
folding in on itself beautifully.

In the hours which Buddha
calls my past, I woke startled
by the vicious barking of the dog.
The doorbell rang. Rain fell in sheets.
A man tapped on the glass.

The fold in the thin gray line,
with lavender and yellow, opened
into a clitoral shape, a place
to rest and be warm. The man,
who was some mother's child,
came from the future to curl up
until help was a certainty.
I think Buddha was smiling
in our future ever so sweetly.

My husband turned the lock.
I waited in the dark on the stairs.
Once inside the man told my husband
the story of his truck
blowing up on the main road.
He had ventured from house to house.
For that small present, we
were interchangeable: one of us
came with a story; one of us stood
in the darkness and one listened.

The mother's child stayed long enough
to use the phone and to ask God to bless us.
He left, crawling out of that place
warmed by the lavender and the yellow,
leaving a turquoise tint behind,
and the colors spread out like electricity
along that endless gray line.

We left a light burning
for the rain-soaked stranger
journeying toward us from the darkness,
who wanted to borrow the thin gray line
for just a moment before we all traveled
on into our pasts. We needed,
the three of us, to meet, however briefly,
on our way to death. The Buddha
smiles in our past, sweetly so.

MOON OVER ALABAMA

Then you were a pretty man named Rusty
with a few tales to tell your grandbabies

and a bunch of us students were riding
on the university bus when somewhere

just this side of Talladega
we started the dares and double dares

Everybody was laughing so hard our sides ached
and the bus bounced southward toward Tuskegee

and over there in the Governor's Mansion
George Wallace thought he was ruling us all

when your eye caught mine and we seized the dare
tore down our jeans and pressed our backsides

up against the rear window of that bus
and you can tell anybody you want

I never would have done it if you had been white
no matter how pretty you were

DEAR M

Do you remember me? I was one of those white children,
the smart-mouthed ones that belonged to Norma Jean.
I was the one you found in your room behind the kitchen,
standing there with your hanging dresses,

next to the Bahama sofa bed, sprung by your weight.
I was willing to wait with you, wait for your escape.
I was afraid of this new house my mama had bought,
my mama who liked warm, soft breezes and cool whiskey.

You came to Florida with us, riding in the backseat.
You thought my mama was pretty but not very nice.
Her children couldn't sleep through a whole tropical night.
We slept with you and you loved our meanness out.

Our days were filled with butterbeans and afternoon rain,
until the day you put on a big yellow hat and he came
in his shiny cab. My mother told her friend Nel
that she should have left you standing in the dirt.

I think of you often and sometimes catch a glimpse of you
or the me that was with you. I feel very proud.
I live in the North now. My knees are round
like yours and my flowers attract butterflies.

ARABIA

I take the depression medication.
Still, when someone speaks to me
in a very direct way, my eyes
fill with tears. Even now,
dreaming of witches and their cats,
I am as cliché as it sounds.

They had cats, I whisper to our cat,
who I notice has grown thin.
I am thinking more about death than I should
and liking the sound of the word *mecca*.
Can a word be a talisman?
Can I ever pull my feet from the sand?

I sit in a chair for hours,
looking out a window at, say, a tree,
choking on embellishment.
Something has my tongue: I consider
the light, my flesh, my next breath.

A sound can taste so good,
better than butter. Sometimes,
I long for the tremble,
I long for the whoosh and the flutter,
to be *mecca*, but I am buried
up to my eyeballs and unbecoming.

BATHING JACK

1.

If you die of this stupid disease,
I'll toast you, slinging my full glass
in your face. You told me I could enjoy it too.
I promise to drop *HOWL*
down your bare spine,
one word at a time,
wash you in mothers' milk.

2.

Before you got sick, Peter found the bear pit
but gave it to you. You took the curious there
to see the rotting cows left as bait.
You loved the notion of hunters baiting bears
and used it to seduce all comers.

As freaky as you,
the end of a double rainbow
plunged into the meadow.
Bathed in its irony,
you jogged through its arch,
returning from the bear pit,
a sweating stranger in tow.

3.

It's raining buckets;
not rum, semen, or urine,
blood, spit, or gasoline,
but cold mountain water.
In the smiling photograph, you
are barbecuing back of the lodge
after the sky opened up.

Any minute you could drown
in the tears of your lovers.

A POEM FOR MY
DALMATIAN TO READ AT SLAMS

I sleep and I eat.
I piss on nature. I piss
on teenage girls when I can.
I hike up my leg and let-er-rip.
I'd like to climb up you, snarling, and
I like to hump, too,
especially Max the Rottweiller
from down the block.
He bites my face
until the blood rises.
I am so happy.

I like rare steak and spotted owl,
but get mostly vegetables.
My pack are good eaters.
I sit in their laps;
they stroke me,
and I lick their faces.
We sleep in the big bed.
I clean their feet,
cleaner than any foot-washing Baptist.
I lie on sofas too and dig them out.
Mostly, I'd like to kill the paper boy.

A PRETTY WOMAN

Despairing, I separate the petals.
I am grieving for this year's last rose.
No, I am afraid my husband will love this woman,
whose skirt brushes my garden when she approaches.
I recognize in her the ancient hag
who stalked other creatures and ate.
I wait with pollen smeared like dried egg yoke
on my cheek. I will not run.
The garden is having a say, and I am still.
Instinct might see me through.

COMMUNITY GARDEN, LAWRENCEVILLE, NEW JERSEY

The voices of cicadas sizzle.
The weight of the well's water
creaks in the Muslim woman's red wagon wheels.
A bee buzzes within a closed squash blossom.
The Chinese couple hoe the earth softly
as with a calligrapher's brush. The garden
is filled with the small sounds of so many breathing.
The man from Trinidad chirps to the tall African
wondering what stinks to high heaven:
My manure is making a lot of noise.

If a place in time is a destination,
I have arrived in a chorus of tongues,
wing beats, and the breeze through stalks of corn.
Here even the dirt speaks, the sun
beats down on us, pulsing like our blood.
I have grown gourds to rattle.

THE WARBLER'S SONG

The emphatic *hurry, hurry, hurry*
over a burst of *Weesee, Weesee, Weesee,*
its name trilled somewhere far off
amid the chatter of *cheery, cheery*
chip chippity swee ditchity tchip cher woo
with you, with you tew, tew, tew we ta woo.

Someone is whistling, whistling
a lispy dreamy *zray zaree, hurry, hurry.*
A male is singing *sweet you, sweet you, sweet chew*
a *buzzy beer, beer, beer, zoo zee zoo zoo*
A female cries, husky and emphatic, *witchy, witchity, witch*
followed by the male's rigorous *see see see it.*

A bright *please, please, pleased to meet you*
teeta teeta teeta teet, the new little voice chants.
She is a girl child *zee up, with you, with you,*
trilling *chip, chippee, sugar sweet, sugar sweet.*
This fine June morning *zray zee zoo*
a female birthed a female *witchity witchy, see it.*

BOY

A great blue heron ambled along the creek.
At next glance, he was transformed
into a boy who strode out onto the road.

Perhaps like the Japanese Crane Maiden,
he was adopted by a couple, long childless,
like my husband and me.

This bird, just become a boy,
just bathed in bright water,
has come into a lather of sunlight.

Other children will sense his difference,
something of the heron, some memory of feathers.
Maybe the gray around his eyes will betray him.

When the curved finger of the new moon
beckons, if he survives into manhood,
he might translate the music

of birds, revealing the meanings.
He could make a song so true
and lucid, we will all be transformed.

III
THEY CARRY
THE STORIES

THE MOTHERS NAME THE CIRCLE

The Birth Mother:
When war was already old and stone circles new,
before you drew your first breath, flint spears killed your dad.
You'll never suck my too-full breasts;
come out, stop hiding, there's druid's milk for you.
I've beaten you and you've nearly drowned.
Listen well: you will eat a fish. A fish will eat you.
I'll beat you again, until you learn to swim.

The Soul:
You hope to fly away and need strong wings;
you've assaulted a wild duck. Let her stay with her clutch.
Let her keep her wings and stay with her clutch.
Let her stay with her clutch and keep one wing.
Let me stay with my clutch. I can fish without wings.
Why do you want my wings? They are dead to you.
Please let me go; I am dead to you.

The Foster Mother:
Casting my line into a well, singing my prophecy,
I saw you swimming in my dream, eating my dream.
I was a fish, roe, gills, and fins.
You must grow a tree in the sea.
You will learn how it is to be fed.
Why have you hidden under a stone, eating raw fish?
A shadow will rise inside you, larger than you, larger still.

The Earth:
I am monstrous, angry, and hungry for you.
I will eat you and stop my pain.
The roots of your tree are piercing my belly.
The well you are digging in my side will kill me.
You are born again in my bile.
You know everything there is to know about dying.

MY ALTITUDE

Female, born not far above sea level
from the small sea of Momma's womb,
I cannot tell where the tide ends and my blood begins.
My heart does not have the muscle
of mountain people, and my skin longs
for moisture. I could slip back into the water in a single beat.
Most things come to rest on my altitude
or roll, fall, or stride through it, wheels, bullets,
and bombs and our bodies at rest. The relics of saints are here,
and sap and rivers run their course.
This is the place where small shiny wings hum,
and there is the rustle of things that scurry.

MY LONGITUDE

isn't a travel destination.
Digging through the earth
would be my path, straight
to Tibet and ready to head south.

Born facing north toward Rock City,
Muncie, and Battle Creek,
child of the Drowning
and Little Current Rivers,
I beg for the Bay
of God's Mercy,
and fear the Fury Strait.
I would not follow
my longitude across
the Arctic Circle and
stretch out into Siberia
or slide into Kazakhstan,
nick the Silk Road,
or mount the Kunlun.

Rather remembering
when I was five and mother harped
about the starving Chinese children
standing upside down and her begging
me to eat my vegetables, I consult
the map and realize
these were little Tibetans;

upon this discovery,
I'd dig straight through
the earth to an unnamed lake
in Tibet, where I wasn't born;
to travel on through Nepal,
and pick up Lakshmi's path
of wealth and good fortune,

pass millions of candles
burning in tiny paper boats
on the Ganges,
to slip into the sea
at the Bay of Bengal.

I might abandon
the journey here,
as navigation depends
on what time it is,
and, at fifty, heading
over the Equator
in the Indian Ocean,
outside the Area of
Optimization
where tears in the map occur,
requires bravery.

There is so much water
and only the moon and the stars
to tell me where I am
until solid ice and ground
at the South Pole
and no land at the Tropic of Capricorn
or the Galápagos,
and once again I face
the Equator at sea.

The Isla del Coco,
the Arenal Volcano,
Mosquitia, Honduras
and my swimming across
the Yucatán Channel
into the Gulf of Mexico
bathing in my mother's ashes

only to climb out
of the ocean at Apalachicola,
pass the Boll Weevil Monument,
heading north to Opelika,
to the place my people
call home. Where I
was born facing north
toward Rock City.

LATITUDINAL

My grandfather left Texas on a cattle boat when he was
thirteen, knowing full well there were four dimensions:
latitude, longitude, altitude, and gender; no fool he. He used
the Southern Cross to find his way. When he crossed the
Equator, the sea was less salty but not his tears.

I was born breech, the umbilical cord round my neck, spit
into my grandfather's hands at thirty-two and three-quarters
degrees north latitude, a world of red clay, piney woods,
hydrangeas, camellias, bougainvillea, magnolia, called
Opelika. I know how to travel feet first.

When my latitude stretched out from me running east over
the place of my lost virginity past Charleston and slipping
through the Sargasso Sea, I pretended to be damaged. The
earth always spinning, I hit land in Morocco and slid under
the Marrakech Express, plunging through the Sahara,
dipping in and out of Homer's wine-dark sea into Palestine.
The roots of the blood orange tree dug into my latitude. It
would be many years before I measured the circumference,
but I would, and marry the son of a Jew, son of a Jew and
so on back to the beginning.

I sailed through more saline sandy deserts into the fertile
crescent; I would never bear my own child. No help from
compasses here, where in the name of family honor, girls are
being murdered. I traced a route through mountains,
Kashmir, high Himalayan peaks, Tibet, where babies are
killed for being born female, past Shanghai, Izu Trench,
Musician's Seamount, over faults where fish with no eyes
swim. I learned to manage ebb and flow.

I was hot and thirsty when I passed through Tijuana and
Mexicali into the desert home stretch, past a Papago
woman holding the baby she loves. I saw cantaloupes

growing in the Pecos and spied the place where my Daddy
would total his car hitting a huge sow near my other
grandfather's house in Louisiana.

I crossed the Mississippi at Tallulah and headed home to
Alabama. On through Eutaw where I joined the NAACP
and my cousin died from a kick in the head from a horse. I
learned that the very same place can house choice or
        happenstance.

I skidded over wet and dry earth, naked, my bones my
sextant, a female born on a dangerous line, trying to
position myself in starlight. On my latitude, men have
thrown acid in women's faces. I cannot fathom why it takes
generations for our skin to adjust to latitude. I was born
full of tears and, like God, I have eyes.

GENDER

Like Alice, I can always open a small door into a new room, surprising
        and perfect. Then
I wake   and am Pandora once more, and my boxes,
        closets, and drawers burst
with evils and filth   the bones of baby mice,
        lovesick amputees
crushed in yellowed tissue   and starving dogs
whining somewhere, deep
        buried in the ruins, every dark secret some rusty
trinket or decaying photograph,
news clippings of obits, suicide, and cancer.

Like Hansel and Gretel's witch, the outside of my house is made
        of candy, all sweets
and pretties   an invitation.   I am caged inside,
        all the children's stories heaped
on me like the bones of the dead. I am small in the corner
of my crammed closet, picking away at the bits of memory and
        skin   with no
place to put them. I am storing my life in my head like
        Akhmatova,   but
with no reason. The pens and pencils strewn around me are useless
        in the dark. I will sleep
more now so I can dream of the air and doors opening onto
        streets and gardens.

I think I am sleeping   even now, and I wake to the ringing
        doorbell and a pounding
to be let in and music. I try to warn of the danger but I have been
        silent too long.
The door opens just a crack, and the bones and dirt rush out,
        an infection. I am   so
ashamed and, through the swirl of wreckage, I see the ones
        who love me catching every
single bit in their bare hands, tearing the largest hunks and stuffing

        garbage bags full. The music
swirls into every cabinet and across the floors.
        It rains,   until
the chaos turns soft, and we dance all night, up close and
        swaying together. At first light, I
open my eyes and my remaining treasures gleam. Everyone
        is laughing and there are small
doors, too many to count, and there is light in every
crack and keyhole. I have been awake the whole time.

THEY HAVE NO MORE
FOR THE LAND

(after Samuel Beckett)

The Crow boy draws a picture of a man,
with a coyote's head, standing under a tree.
On the shelf I have two other drawings:
Coyote as an old man under a tree
and Red Woman, his wife, at night;
in dim light, under no moon, she is watching
her husband hide in the old stories.
The tree bows and scrapes and talks crazy.

There are claps of thunder and howling
because I have come to make the stories mine.
Coyote is dying, his legs are rubbery from old bullet wounds.
I nurse the bruises on my ribs.
More claps of thunder and weak cries.
Red Woman, Coyote's wife, sits with the stars.
She is above my eyes. We have said goodbye here before.
Today, again, the wind drives the tree mad.

The stars blow off the shelf.
They have no more for the land.
There is little rain. The sky is too clear.
In the beginning just doesn't say enough.
The Crow boy calls Coyote grandfather.
Coyote's heart was always too close to his skin.
He was always panting, panting always.

GONERIL'S SUBTEXT

Shakespeare's play grew on us like nails and hair.
Dad likes the story where we turn into swans best.
Yes, I'm talking to you! You
sitting in a theater, watching us.

Word has just come of my sister, Regan.
Poor thing, in her lacy bodice of pretty words,
dying, her chest filled with poison.

I adjusted my bobbin-net cap
to cover the soft spots in my skull,
looked sweet as sugar and fed it to her.
I couldn't have her putting a finger into my brain.
Don't you be so distant and smug.
Someone could come in from the lobby
and shoot you in the back of the head.
Stop your moaning.
Too bad, there isn't a single story about you becoming a swan.

You could be the one in the library,
reading the part where Dad carries Cordelia on stage,
so dead, with her Chantilly mouth and genuine eyes.
Some other kid could come in and spray bullets
through your chest and arms. I get hung.

AS FAR AS THE EYE CAN SEE

If I could, I would stand in a great golden field
while the wheat waves under a cloudless blue,
but the generosity would slam me to my knees.

My father farmed pigs and chickens
and grew only vegetables.
He chose to live life close to his skin
and fear God. These days
he worries I don't visit him
because he was stingy when I was a girl.

I have forgotten the bride's name,
only remembering that she was French.
I recall that her father cherished her.
He grew her a sea of sunflowers
as her wedding gift. It stretched,
under an expanse of white sky,
like thousands of guests in yellow hats,
far into the dark of a sloe night.

Did father and child revel in unbroken vistas?
Perhaps the distance between them
and the horizon was wieldy mostly.

My brother shows me a picture
of my father as an old man.
I always imagined him young,
the one who wanted to give me away.
I saved him the trouble by leaving,
eyes focused on the vanishing point.

Did the bride and groom honeymoon on an ocean?
Did they settle in a sandy desert
and did she watch it shift like water,
or like her field in the wind?
Did her father come to visit her there?

Sunflowers volunteer in my garden
and grow gangly into differing heights.
They spend their summer nodding at passersby.
In September they bow their heavy heads,
tired of waiting for my father.
Their prayers rise up well into the winter.

But for the vertigo and blinding anger,
I would walk across a snow-covered plain,
each tiny crystal of ice glistening
like a diamond, dazzling my eyes.

WHEN J TOLD ME
HER OLD ENEMY WAS DYING

I thought of mine whom I treat with due respect
though I do not always love her
though I tell her I do.
I treat her kindly
for my own sake,
not hers.

My old enemy didn't come to my wedding,
wishes I had never been born,
and told us children
never to have any,
and we obliged.

My old enemy told me I would recognize her wisdom,
understand that blood is thicker than water
and her willingness to have died for me,
when I grew up and had the children
I would never have.

My old enemy says her mother was the best,
though when we buried her
on a beautiful May day,
there were ten of us,
one an historian.

My old enemy savors her memories,
altering us to suit her,
telling and retelling
her pretty fictions
until we beg her
to be quiet.

I wait for this lightning to strike.
My old enemy is old and sick
and I will miss her so
when she finally stops
breathing the air
I breathe.

WEAVING A HORSE

When I was a child, fairies clung to me.
We ate meals cooked by a blind woman named Tyla
and watched tadpoles and caterpillars metamorphose
as the earth inhaled and the tide ebbed.

Now I am one who unravels. I am wounded.
My Fates continue their weaving,
never allowing me to dream with scissors.
The sound of his breathing came first,

the horse running in a perfect field.
I was breathless with admiration, *moon-cipher*,
was *rain-word*, made in the whir of a spinning wheel.
I learned how a thing is made thread by thread.

The stars were once angels and the planets
endowed with reason. My two eyes are round
like the earth but they have grown to look out not in.
Most girls long to ride the beast. I longed

to wear the horse like a garment, to see
fantastic worlds through the globes of his eyes.
I would become the horse thread by thread.
I would love myself. I would become the thing I loved.

If you love something enough, surely it will love you.
I am nearly fifty and there are more days than not
when I am indecipherable. Birds try to catch my meaning.
I long to lick the edge of heaven with a fiery tongue.

I could throw off my hair shirt and stop pitying myself.
Thread by thread, I am becoming the horse's ass.
I will look into my lover's eyes. I think they are blue
as the sky into which they gaze. They see me too.

SINCE SHE DIED

I notate the grief in hollows of my body
where music comes from.

In finally-summer, the thousand leaves
chatter on a magnolia tree.

Enough of any small moving thing
will make a sound, just as the monarchs'

wings sing while they flutter
off the trees of their Mexican home.

If enough spiders gathered,
could we hear them spin silk?

One drop of rain falls;
the storm is deafening. No one heard

the last rattle of her lungs. Not I
who lived in her and know the melody

of her blood.

GONE

Today,
the sun arrived.
You didn't see it.
You're just one more cracker, dead at age forty-four.

But when we were sixteen,
my mom loved you.
You were a football hero,
a good thing because you needed all that bulk
to sling my butt
into your father's station wagon

one night under a full moon. I was typically,
Saturday-night, knee-crawling drunk.
You found me basking on the beach,
waxing to my best friend Cindy about the phosphorescence.

When you finally got me home,
I woke up the whole neighborhood,
so smashed, I staggered
into the house across the street.

I smoked weed too; you didn't, except once to please me.
You started going on about the cells in our bodies,
how each one was a tiny universe
filled with people just like us,
and how we lived in the single cell of a larger person.
I thought, *I'm never going to smoke with this bozo again.*

I didn't,
thinking you needed every single brain cell you had
just to get by as a normal person.
As I got out of the car you were still pontificating,
saying, *And so on to infinity.*

So sweet
as I think back on it,
you were just sweet, too sweet.

Last night, I didn't sleep much.
The afternoon mail came
with your obituary.
They come a few a year now
from my mom. Suicide is big,
drug-related deaths like yours, and drunk driving.
One of our classmates was killed by her husband.
I look forward to the day someone dies of natural causes.

And so on to infinity, you said.
Twenty-eight years ago as I was walking away from you,
the last thing I heard you say was, *And so on to infinity.*
In both directions, I hope.

OTHER BOYS ARE PROTECTED BY A GREEN DRAGON

But his mother is an angry wind, the force
whipping from her mouth into his. If he tries
to protest, his body fills with her.

Their chimney fights with the sky. A craving
wolf claws at their door. Arrested
again, barely thirteen. No immortals

ride by on elephants, just a tangled
mother spewing wind, foreshadowing the glint
of a bullet buried in flesh. If the frog

had spit a pearl through any other door, this boy
would be luminous as a paper lantern,
as yang as the moon hanging on a golden

hook. Tonight the boy spins slowly
down our front walk like oily smoke
with despair's tongue down his throat.

He spies me in our round window slick with rain.
His mother will be audible soon, the echoes
of countless cruelties gathering in her chest.

RESONANCE

(for Julie)

The air was delicious with gardenias
on those long-ago summer nights
when I began to learn of death,
lying in the grass, my loved ones
and I gazing up at the stars.
Fox fire glowed in the near woods.
In the darkness, we murmured
to each other, as our kind has
since we first tasted air.

The dirt-daubers slept in their caves,
tiny under the summer house's eaves.
I asked no one in particular
to tell of Big Mama and the pig.
The words exhaled like breath.
Audible, they hung in the air
with laughter simmering nearby.
This is my family's way, to curl up
with our dogs and, in deep gulps,
inhale our ancestors' lives.

I was thinking of this when John
died today, as his breathing slowed
and he let out his last tender breath,
as it lingered in the sickroom
until it could nest in your hair.
When you begin to shake your head,
when you shake it in disbelief,
listen for the tiny echoes like changing.
They carry the stories of his blood.

AT THE MUSE'S SWIMMING POOL

My mother's ashes on my tongue,
tasting tears, I drift with the water,
on my back. In my ear,
the muse whispers Rumi,
and what I taste is not salt
but Persia. It is night, all
I know of my mother swims in me here,
all ages, all selves.

When I look again, my many mothers
are dancing, ecstatic, their feet and ankles
are shiny as they spin past me,
the surface of the pool rippling out
in a thousand circles until the muse
scoops them up for us to wear on our fingers,
rings of star sapphires and pearly desert moons.

HALLOWEEN IN THE
HIGH MOUNTAIN DESERT

Gladys asked me to stay until night
when all the colors of the earth gathered,
not ghosts or witches but colors.
Each year, she filled her pumpkin patch
with giant creatures fashioned
from wire and dyed feathers, sort-of elephants,
cows, dinosaurs, giraffes, and buffalo.
I wondered why she made no birds.

Once I knew three witches
all called Jane, the heaviest one
loved to cast spells, hence the altars
to Lilith, Colette, and the Holy Mother.
I spent the night in their attic
with their sacred oils and animal-shaped candles
for making magic. More than anything they wanted to fly.

Gladys wouldn't have known Colette from cabbage.
Gladys Bickkelhaupt raised chickens,
and over the years there were so many feathers.
With a couple of shots of bourbon in my belly,
I spent the afternoon dancing around her pumpkins
trying to keep my feet warm and making wishes.

Carloads of children came and went.
The air quivered with infinity times three.
At moonrise, I thought of remaining there forever,
dancing in a feather dress. The moon was gigantic and orange
over the fuchsia buffalo and the cow
as blue as the ocean of my own childhood.
There were so many feathers, a lifetime of them.
All things are possible, a turquoise tiger told me
just before he unfurled his wings.

SELKIE

Mother's ashes poured onto the sea,
we trolled back and forth in the flashing water.

In the old house, on the shore, upstairs
in the corner bedroom,

pale blue-green plaster caressed
by the water's painterly fingers.

I wheezed, my chest rattled, the curtains
rippled like lungs and sea bladders.

In the night, high tide etched the walls
with indecipherable messages; bubbles popped,

more like blisters than language. I breathe
like my mother now,

but I will need gills to find her again.

CAT FISHING

Diving from the roof of Uncle Homer and Aunt May's houseboat
into the backwater, I am live as lightning;
my ten-year-old bones and flesh strike the dark lake,
and I gulp the sweet cold flavors of cedar, algae, and pine.

Like some Mel Blanc cartoon, even the snakes wiggle and sing.
But not in the black winter, forty years later
when we bring our daddy here, all the blood
and beer burned from his body. We will pour him

overboard, he will disappear quick as the lick of a flame.
When the song of fire and water hisses and sighs.
We will be the living, as our father's ashes far below
finally settle on the whiskers of the one that got away.

I do not know where his soul is now. He once told me
God is everywhere. I wrap each word in hot breath;
loved, I, love, half sent in bottles, the rest set sailing
on paper boats. Love burns blinding bright, cast upon the water.